GIDS Analysis

edited by | herausgegeben von

Stefan Bayer
Burkhard Meißner
Matthias Rogg
Gary Schaal
Jörn Thießen

Volume 5 | Band 5

Klaus B. Beckmann | Lennart Reimer

An Enquiry Into
Linear Conflict Models

The **Deutsche Nationalbibliothek** lists this publication in the
Deutsche Nationalbibliografie; detailed bibliographic data
are available on the Internet at http://dnb.d-nb.de
ISBN   978-3-8487-7156-1 (Print)
           978-3-7489-1208-8 (ePDF)

British Library Cataloguing-in-Publication Data
A catalogue record for this book is available from the British Library.
ISBN   978-3-8487-7156-1 (Print)
           978-3-7489-1208-8 (ePDF)

Library of Congress Cataloging-in-Publication Data
Beckmann, Klaus B. / Reimer, Lennart
An Enquiry Into Linear Conflict Models
Klaus B. Beckmann / Lennart Reimer
60 pp.
Includes bibliographic references and index.
ISBN   978-3-8487-7156-1 (Print)
           978-3-7489-1208-8 (ePDF)

Onlineversion
Nomos eLibrary

1st Edition 2021
© Nomos Verlagsgesellschaft, Baden-Baden, Germany 2021. Overall responsibility
for manufacturing (printing and production) lies with Nomos Verlagsgesellschaft mbH
& Co. KG.

Preface

The German Institute for Defence and Strategic Studies (GIDS) is on a mission to improve the quality of strategic studies in Germany in both an academic and a consulting dimension. This mission is relevant because the field has been neglected by German academics as well as by the German military community for understandable historical reasons. Military strategy and operational art used to smack too much of the old *Generalstab* for post-war Germans, and consequently this field was regarded as unpalatable and as a politically unacceptable subject matter for academic research.

The result of this is a dearth of strategic thinking in our country. Interestingly, this historical development has also spawned a peculiar German specialisation on *Friedens- und Konfliktforschung* that emphasises the *avoidance* of conflict, and which largely replaces the traditional field of strategic studies in Germany.

The authors of this monograph admit to be firmly rooted in the strategic studies camp. For once conflict has become inevitable, we want our side to persevere. This implies that we should try to understand conflict primarily with a view to *win* it, and that recommendations on how nations can pursue their self-interest with an expectation of success are an important objective of scientific study. In the final analysis, our credible ability to win will also help to deter conflict in the first place.

It is the role of HSU / UniBw H to contribute fundamental research to the joint effort with *Führungsakademie* that is the GIDS. We suggest to begin this part of our common task by reviewing, and by extending, the various theoretical approaches to conflict modelling that exist in the previous literature. This is the task that our team took up when we switched our main effort in research from the economics of corruption and tax evasion to conflict economics and began to engage heavily in teaching the German war college Master "Militärische Führung und Internationale Sicherheit" (MFIS).

Beckmann's appointment as President of HSU / UniBw H in April 2018 led to a disruption in this work. We therefore decided to consolidate the existing material and develop it into a series of monographs in order to document our results – incomplete as the may be – and to make them available in the context of GIDS research and beyond. The present small volume is the first result of this effort. It deals with classical models in the tradition of Lanchester (1916, 1956) and Richardson (1919) that do not take agents to be optimising, but accept this restriction in order to tell a dynamic story that is very hard to establish in differential game (Lee, 2007; Isaacs, 1965) methods. We also link this argument to a proposal on how differential game analysis might be transformed to address these practicality concerns.

The present booklet combines several hitherto unpublished working papers from the last few years. The material has been rearranged, heavily revised and extended for presentation in book form. We sincerely hope that this little monograph will prove useful and further the debate at the GIDS.

Hamburg, December 16, 2020

Klaus Beckmann
Lennart Reimer

Contents

Contents

List of Figures

List of Tables

11

Chapter 1: Introduction

For static models of conflict, there exist several classifications that are based on taxonomies of 2 × 2 ordinal games. After Schelling (1960) distinguished between zero-sum and mixed motive games, the seminal work by Rapoport and Guyer (Rapoport and Guyer, 1966; Rapoport et al., 1976) provided a full taxonomy of all these games. Brams (2011, 1994) later proposed an alternative version. While the first classifications relied on the strategic properties of the various game forms, recent work tends to emphasise topological arrangements of games based on similarities between them (Robinson and Goforth, 2005; Perlo-Freeman, 2006; Bruns, 2010).

It is tempting to try and develop a comparably simple approach to *the classification of conflict dynamics*. Our approach is to employ a general version of the traditional linear (two-party) differential equation models in the Lanchester (1916, 1956), Richardson (1919, 1960a) and Lotka-Volterra traditions. In contrast to game theory (in particular, differential games), such models use first-order linear differential equations without explicit optimisation. This continues to be a standard technique in analyses of military conflict (Biddle, 2004) and combat modelling (Washburn and Kress, 2009).[1] Such models are also applied to conflicts beyond military attrition in the narrow sense: for example, Atkinson et al. (2012) look at the chances of success of revolts using a Lanchester-type model, and Francisco (2009) applies the Lotka-Volterra equations to data on internal protest and repression across a broad range of countries, including democratic ones. Schramm and Gaver (2013) combine a Lanchester model with an epidemological approach – itself a special case of our type of model – to model the impact of hacker attacks in a war of attrition.

---

1 Mainstream models in conflict economics build on the rent-seeking literature (Congleton et al., 2008) to determine optimal effort levels of agents engaged in conflict. This literature is reviewed in Garfinkel and Skaperdas (2007). Both approaches could be combined by setting up a differential game or, if this is mathematically unfeasible, by considering a form of bounded rationality where agents determine the response that would be optimal in a static setting – given the current values of the state and control variables – and then close a certain percentage of the gap between their current control and this "optimal" value (Baker and Bulte, 2005; Frey and Rohner, 2007; Beckmann and Reimer, 2014).

It has long been recognised that these linear models are related and that their coefficients may be used to distinguish particular situations (see, for example, Protopopescu et al., 1987). Our study adds to the literature in that is states the general model systematically and provides an empirical application to *phases of conflict*. Such phases are primarily classified by the combination of (statistically significant) signs on the parameters of three terms in the differential equations describing the general model. In addition, empirical estimates for parameters can be used to distinguished between phases based on their *stability properties*. That, in a nutshell, is the overarching goal of the present monograph.

We begin by describing a general linear conflict model for the two-party case theoretically (chapter 2). We argue that this model comprises the large majority of two-party interactions discussed in the literature – such as Lanchester, Boulding-Richards, and Lotka-Volterra – as special cases, and that it consists of simple building blocks that can be accorded strategic meaning. In chapter 3, one special case is then singled out, namely the Richardson (1919) equations describing arms races, which were extended in monographs published posthumously (Richardson, 1960a,b), and which Boulding (1962) applied in a psychological context.[2] In contrast to the Lanchester and Lotka-Volterra models, however, this model has not received any attention in the recent literature, although it is still popular as an example for teaching differential equations.[3] The third chapter also contains some extensions for Richardson's original model. We then build on Boulding (1962) to present a psychological interpretation of the Richardson equations, which we extend to the three-party case (chapter 4). The stability properties of the extended Boulding model are explored using numerical experimentation.

We then turn to the empirical application of the general linear model from chapter 2. Chapter 5 explores two approaches, one of them relying on a time series analysis of GDELT[4] data from the Ethiopoan-Eritreian war, the other attempting to estimate the parameters of the differential equation model by using structural equation model techniques. The latter part of chapter 5 is closely related to Francisco (2009). In fact, we use the same data set as

---

2 Lewis Fry Richardson is little known in economics, and without the work of his fellow Quaker Boulding his work may not have resounded in our field at all. He is, however, well remembered for his contributions to other disciplines. On this, see Hunt (1995).

3 In mathematics, Richardson's equations are a popular simple model of conflict, which amongst other things is used in the classroom to explain phase diagramming, see https://www.youtube.com/watch?v=e3FfmXtkppM (last checked on Dec 16th, 2020). The recent conflict economics text by Anderton and Carter (2009) also has a section on the Richardson model.

4 See https://www.gdeltproject.org/about.html (last checked on Dec 16th, 2020).

Francisco (2009), but with the full model including all direct and interaction effects. We also provide estimates for different conflict scenarios to illustrate that our approach can indeed be used as a basis for classification. However, we confine our analysis to some example countries.

Finally, we also consider how the gulf between parametrical and optimising models of behavior in conflict might be bridged (chapter 6). For this purpose, we generalise an adaptive, myopic boundedly rational approach to decision-making that we used previously in Beckmann and Reimer (2014).

Chapter 2: A general linear conflict model for the two-party case

Let x (y) be a state variable denoting some measure of aggression for party x (y) in a two-agent conflict.[1] Its time derivative $\dot{x}$ ($\dot{y}$) represents the current (de-) escalation of conflict and depends on the values of the state variables according to the system of equations below:

$$\dot{x} = \alpha_1(\hat{x} - x) + \alpha_2 y + \alpha_3 xy \qquad (2.1)$$

$$\dot{y} = \beta_1(\hat{y} - y) + \beta_2 x + \beta_3 yx \qquad (2.2)$$

The three terms in equations (2.1) and (2.2) are the standard components that make up all the traditional models. Listed in the order of their indices, they are the following:

1. A *growth effect*. If $\hat{x} = \hat{y} = 0$ and $\alpha_1, \beta_1 < 0$, this term models exponential growth in the state variable. If, on the other hand, $\alpha_1, \beta_1 > 0$, it captures an asymptotic approach to the limits $\hat{x}$ and $\hat{y}$ (which may be zero).
2. A *reaction effect*. This measures x's (y's) escalation as a result of the other party's state variable; if $\alpha_2, \beta_2 < 0$, it can also – as in Lanchester's "square law" (MacKay, 2006) – represent a party's losses from aimed fire by its opponent's forces.
3. An *interaction effect*. In predator-prey models, such an effect typically comes about as predators' reproductive success depends on both their own numbers and the abundance of prey to feed on, in attrition models, it captures the effect of indirect fire.

Note that an extension to three (or more) parties is straightforward as long as only two-way interaction terms are allowed. Intriligator and Brito (1988, 1990)'s model of guerrilla warfare, for instance, links the number of insurgents x, the number of security personnel y and the population under insurgent control z as follows:

---

1 In Lanchester (1916)'s original model, x represented the number of aircraft fielded by one side in a theatre, in Richardson (1960a)'s model, armament levels, in the Lotka-Volterra version, populations of competing species. Boulding (1962) added a psychological interpretation. We are not prepared to argue that the model works equally well in all of these applications – in fact, one of the objectives of empirical estimation of it using different data sets can be to find out where the limits of application are.

$$\dot{x} = a_1 xz - a_2 xy \qquad (2.3)$$
$$\dot{y} = b_1 y - b_2 xy \qquad (2.4)$$
$$\dot{z} = c_1 x - c_2 y \qquad (2.5)$$

An important model in epidemiology is the SIR model (Schramm and Gaver, 2013), which splits a constant population into susceptible s, recovered r and infected i people and links the groups using the following equations:

$$\dot{s} = -a_1 si \qquad (2.6)$$
$$\dot{i} = a_1 si - a_2 i \qquad (2.7)$$
$$\dot{r} = a_2 i \qquad (2.8)$$

It is obvious that our three main building blocks are again sufficient to set up these special cases. For the remainder of this paper, however, we will focus on the two-agent case described by equations (2.1) and (2.2). Table 2.1 on page 18 below gives an overview of the most important special cases from the conflict literature and their respective parameter configurations.

Table 2.1: A synopsis of two-party differential equation models

Model	$\hat{x}$	α_1	α_2	α_3	$\hat{y}$	β_1	β_2	β_3
Lanchester ("Square law")	0	0	< 0	0	0	0	< 0	0
Lanchester ("Linear law")	0	0	0	< 0	0	0	0	< 0
Richardson	> 0	< 0	> 0	0	> 0	< 0	> 0	0
Lotka-Volterra (x is prey)	0	> 0	0	< 0	0	< 0	0	> 0

It is straightforward if tedious to obtain a solution for our general model. First, letting $\dot{x} = \dot{y} = 0$ and solving (2.1) and (2.2), we obtain a candidate solution for a steady state in the model:

$$x^* = \pm \frac{1}{2(r_{yx}\xi_{xy} + n_x\xi_{yx})}(n_x n_y - r_{xy}r_{yx} + n_x\hat{x}\xi_{yx} - n_y\hat{y}\xi_{xy} + A) \qquad (2.9)$$

$$y^* = \pm \frac{1}{2(r_{xy}\xi_{yx} + n_y\xi_{xy})}(n_x n_y - r_{xy}r_{yx} + n_x\hat{x}\xi_{yx} - n_y\hat{y}\xi_{xy} + A) \qquad (2.10)$$

where

$$A = \sqrt{-4(r_{yx}\xi_{xy} + n_x\xi_{yx})(n_xn_y\hat{x} + n_yr_{xy}\hat{y}) + (-n_xn_y + r_{xy}r_{yx} - n_x\hat{x}\xi_{yx} + n_y\hat{y}\xi_{xy})^2}$$

While (2.9) and (2.10) appear complicated, note that many terms in these equation will be zero for the special cases of our model. For example, if there is no "aspiration level" – i.e., $\hat{x} = \hat{y} = 0$ –, A simplifies to $\sqrt{r_{xy}r_{yx} - n_xn_y}$.

Regarding the stability properties of the above equilibrium, consider the Jacobian

$$J = \begin{pmatrix} -n_x + \xi_{xy}y & r_{xy} + \xi_{xy}x \\ r_{yx} + \xi_{yx}y & -n_y + \xi_{yx}x \end{pmatrix}$$

whose eigenvalues are given by the solutions to the following characteristic equation:

$$\lambda^2 + \lambda(n_x + n_y - \xi_{yx}x - \xi_{xy}y)$$
$$+n_xn_y - r_{xy}r_{yx} - r_{xy}\xi_{yx}y - r_{yx}\xi_{xy}x - n_x\xi_{yx}x - n_y\xi_{xy}y = 0 \qquad (2.11)$$

Depending on the specific parameters, this general model allows for all possible stability properties. To remind the reader, a stationary point (x^*, y^*) is asymptotically stable if the real parts of both solutions for (2.11) are negative, it is unstable if both those eigenvalues are positive, and saddle point stable if their signs differ. Furthermore, the system will exhibit oscillating behaviour if there is at least one complex eigenvalue.

Finally, there are two special cases:

1. If the real parts of both eigenvalues are zero, we obtain a limit cycle.
2. If there is just one solution to (2.11), we obtain a degenerate node.

Various examples for the different configurations and system behaviours will be presented as we discuss special cases of our model later in this book. The general model itself will be taken up in the empirical chapter 5.

Chapter 3: Special case: the Richardson equations in two dimensions

Richardson (1919) conceived of his equations as a model of an arms race (see also Anderton and Carter, 2009, pp. 199-202). In Boulding (1962)'s version, the equations describe the joint dynamics of the *aggressiveness* (or escalation level) of two parties to a conflict. We will use both stories interchangeably at first, but return to the difference between the two at a later point.

A. Richardson's original equations

Denote by a (b) a measure of party A's (B's) armament, or aggressiveness towards the other, and assume that without interaction, this reverts over time to a base level $\hat{a}$ $(\hat{b})$. In an arms race model, this level would correspond to the desired spending on defence in absence of the relations with the adversary. This base level is, however, not the long-term equilibrium because of the interaction effect: each party's aggressiveness increases exponentially as a function of the competitor's escalation measure. Together with the assumption $a, b > 0$, this gives the Richardson equations

$$\dot{a} = k_a(\hat{a} - a) + r_a b \tag{3.1}$$

$$\dot{b} = k_b(\hat{b} - b) + r_b a \tag{3.2}$$

where the strictly positive parameters k_i and r_i represent the parties' speed of adjustment to the base level and sensitivity to aggression, respectively.

We can explicitly solve this system of linear ODEs for the time paths $a(t), b(t)$ of aggressiveness. For example, in the symmetric case where $r_a = r_b = r$ and $k_a = k_b = k$ (assuming $r \neq k$), we find

$$a(t) = \frac{k(\hat{a}k + \hat{b}r)}{k^2 - r^2} + e^{-kt}(c_1 \cosh(tr) + c_2 \sinh(tr)) \tag{3.3}$$

where c_1 and c_2 are constants. If we additionally assume that $a(0) = b(0) = 0$, we have

$$a(t) = \frac{e^{2rt} - e^{(k+r)t}}{\frac{r-k}{k}e^{(k+r)t}} \hat{a} \tag{3.4}$$

21

and likewise for b.

However, the general properties of this model are better studied using phase diagramme techniques. Letting $\dot{a} = 0$ and $\dot{b} = 0$, we obtain the "nullclines" where the vector field is vertical and horizontal, respectively (written as functions of a for easier plotting)

$$b = \frac{k_a}{r_a}(a - \hat{a}) \tag{3.5}$$

$$b = \hat{b} + \frac{r_b}{k_b}a \tag{3.6}$$

Note that both graphs are upward sloping lines in (a, b)-space and that the equation for $\dot{a} = 0$ has a negative intercept on the b axis, while the other cuts the ordinate at $\hat{b} > 0$. This already implies that there are just two possible configurations (see figure 1). If $\frac{k_a}{r_a} > \frac{r_b}{k_b}$, the two lines intersect in the positive orthant (left-hand panel in figure 1) and there exists a stable stationary equilibrium at

$$(a^*, b^*) = \left(\frac{k_b(\hat{a}k_a + \hat{b}r_b)}{k_ak_b - r_ar_b}, \frac{k_a(\hat{b}k_b + \hat{a}r_b)}{k_ak_b - r_ar_b} \right) \tag{3.7}$$

Otherwise, there is no such intersection and aggressiveness explodes in the positive orthant (right-hand panel in figure 1).

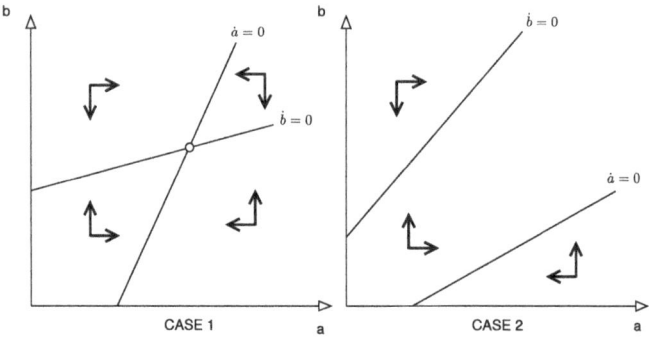

Figure 3.1: The two possible scenarios in the standard Richardson model

Formally, note that the Jacobian for the system (3.1) and (3.2) is

$$J = \begin{pmatrix} -k_a & r_a \\ r_b & -k_b \end{pmatrix}$$

with the two eigenvalues $\lambda_{1,2} = -\frac{1}{2}(k_a + k_b \pm \sqrt{(k_a - k_b)^2 + 4r_a r_b})$. As the term under the square root must be positive given our assumptions, both eigenvalues are real. The obvious condition for both eigenvalues to be *negative* is

$$k_a + k_b > \sqrt{(k_a - k_b)^2 + 4r_a r_b}$$

Square both sides of this inequality and rearrange to find $k_a k_b > r_a r_b$, which is equivalent to the graphical restriction on slopes given earlier as a condition for stability. If this inequality does not hold, we will have two real eigenvalues with differing signs, i.e. saddlepoint stability (however, the equilibrium will be in the negative orthant).

The endless escalation of conflict in this case (2) may appear implausible because infinite aggression levels are an unwieldy concept. However, in interpreting the model, one can assume that there exists a threshold level of escalation beyond which the conflict in question changes its nature (i.e., an open outbreak of military hostilities). One can also add an additional constraint to the model – for instance, a and b could represent the *share* of two competing news media (total broadcast time or pages in a magazine) devoted to a particular conflict, or a particular scandal. The latter modification would give rise to a stable corner solution.

We now propose two variants of the two-agent Richardson model, which we explore in turn:

1. a version which incorporates the idea that it may be escalation rather than the stock of aggressiveness which determines the interaction effect,
2. a model which replaces the deterministic interaction effect with a probabilistic version, taking account of Clausewitzian friction and other sources of uncertainty.

B. An incrementalist Richardson model

In our first variation, we recognise that it can be the *change* in enemy aggression levels, i.e. the *escalation* of conflict, which drives conflict dynamics. We retain the assumption that aggression levels will return to base values $\hat{a}, \hat{b}$ over time, but replace the stock levels of aggression with their time derivatives $\dot{a}, \dot{b}$. This leads to the following model:

$$\dot{a} = k_a(\hat{a} - a) + r_a \dot{b} \tag{3.8}$$

$$\dot{b} = k_b(\hat{b} - b) + r_b\dot{a} \tag{3.9}$$

As was the case for the baseline model, we can solve this system of differential equations explicitly, obtaining complete time paths for the two variables of interest, given the parameters and starting values $a(0), b(0)$. Using the symmetric example from section above, we find

$$a(t) = \left(1 - e^{\frac{k(1+r)t}{r^2-1}}\right)a(0) \tag{3.10}$$

with an analogous solution for b. Again, however, we find it more instructive to take a conventional approach using phase diagrammes to illustrate system behaviour over time for more general parameter values.

Substituting $\dot{b}$ into the first equation of the model and rearranging, we can express the change in a and in b as a function of the state variables

$$\dot{a} = \frac{k_a(\hat{a} - a) + r_ak_b(\hat{b} - b)}{1 - r_ar_b} \tag{3.11}$$

$$\dot{b} = \frac{k_b(\hat{b} - b) + r_bk_a(\hat{a} - a)}{1 - r_ar_b} \tag{3.12}$$

Proceeding as before, we obtain the following equations for the nullclines:

$$b = \frac{\hat{a}k_a + \hat{b}k_br_a - k_aa}{k_br_a} \tag{3.13}$$

$$b = \frac{\hat{b}k_b + \hat{a}k_ar_b - k_ar_ba}{k_br_a} \tag{3.14}$$

Solving this simple system yields the stationary point at $a^* = \hat{a} \wedge b^* = \hat{b}$. This implies that contrary to the standard B-R model, the stationary point always lies in the positive orthant.

For a graphical analysis, observe that the slope of the graph for $\dot{a} = 0$ is steeper than the other iff $r_b < 1$. Also note that the denominator in both equations of motion (3.11) and (3.12) becomes *negative* for $r_ar_b > 1$. All in all, this leaves us with four possible dynamic configurations shown in figure 2. Case 1 exhibits a stable stationary state, whereas case 2 is characterised by instability. However, case 2 differs from the unstable case in the original model in that a corner solution at the origin is also a possibility. Cases 3 and 4 – where $r_b > 1$ – have saddlepoint stable equilibria.

Start from equations (3.11) and (3.12) to find the Jacobian

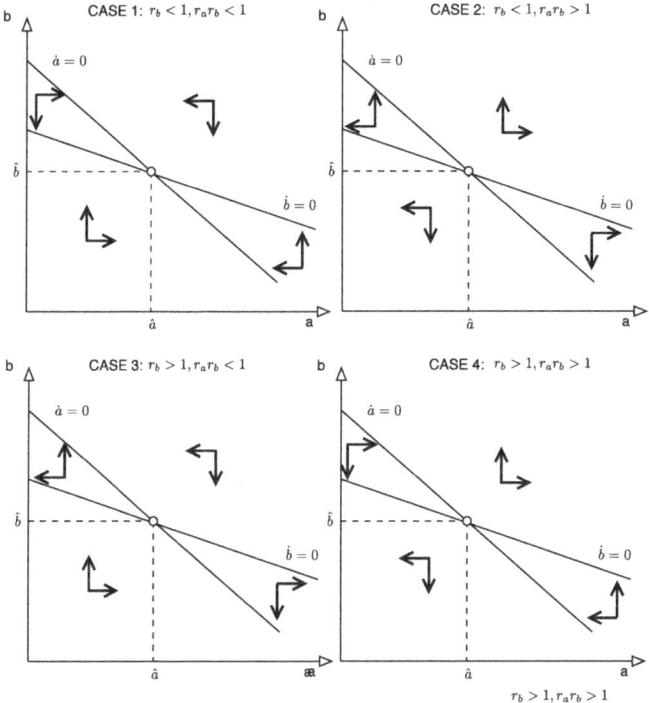

Figure 3.2: The four scenarios in the incrementalist Richardson model

$$J = \begin{pmatrix} -\frac{k_a}{1-r_a r_b} & -\frac{r_a k_b}{1-r_a r_b} \\ -\frac{r_b k_a}{1-r_a r_b} & -\frac{k_b}{1-r_a r_b} \end{pmatrix}$$

and the two eigenvalues $\lambda_{1,2} = \frac{k_a + k_b \pm \sqrt{(k_a - k_b)^2 + 4k_a k_b r_a r_b}}{2r_a r_b - 2}$. While we can rule out complex eigenvalues again, the fact that the sign of the denominator reverses at $r_a r_b = 1$ now gives rise to a total of four possible configurations, as shown in figure 3.2.

In the original Richardson model, it was the *relative* size of adaptation k and reaction coefficients r that determined the dynamic pattern of conflict. Now, it is the *absolute* value of the reaction coefficients alone that proves crucial. It is sufficient for convergence to a stable equilibrium at the "normal" aggro level $\hat{a}, \hat{b}$ that both parties do not respond "in kind" to an enemy escalation, but with an $r < 1$. This feature of the model appears more plausible than the results we obtained for the original formulation. In addition, the incrementalist model allows for a "pacifist" party (with low r) to compensate for the existence of an aggressive opponent in a very plausible manner.

C. Probabilistic interaction

Finally, let us briefly consider how to incorporate *randomness* – and Clause-witzian "friction" – into the simple framework. As a large conflict unfolds, there will be several small interactions during which either side can either escalate, de-escalate, or ignore the other side's aggression. Let a's probability p of escalation depend on b's aggro level according to a probability function $p(b)$ with $p' > 0$ and vice versa. For a large number of such interactions per unit of time, the equations of motion can then be amended by just plugging in the probability functions for $r_a b$ and $r_b a$, respectively. We then obtain the following system of equations

$$\dot{a} = k_a(\hat{a} - a) + s_a p(b) - s_a(1 - p(b)) \tag{3.15}$$

$$\dot{b} = k_b(\hat{b} - b) + s_b p(a) - s_b(1 - p(a)) \tag{3.16}$$

where the s_i represent party i's "step size" of (de-)escalation, assumed to be a constant for simplicity.

We require a specific probability function for plotting or explicit solutions, although basic phase diagrammes such as the ones in figures 1 and 2 could by derived with just some assumptions regarding the curvature of p. Borrowing from the literature on conflict success functions,[1] we employ a *logistic function*

$$p(a) = \frac{1}{1 + e^{\kappa(\hat{a}-a)}} \tag{3.17}$$

where $\hat{a}$ denotes the reference level of aggression by A (i.e., the level where escalation and de-escalation are just as likely), and the parameter κ determines the steepness of the probability function.

One important difference from the variants discussed previously is that the isoclines for $\dot{a}, \dot{b} = 0$ are now non-linear. Also, the fact that the limits of the logistic function are zero for $a, b \to -\infty$ and one for $a, b \to +\infty$ together with the structure of the system imply that there exists a stable intersection in the positive orthant.

---

1 The classic treatment is the book by Hirshleifer (2001).

Chapter 4: Richardson-type conflict between three parties

A. Extension of the basic model to three parties

Consider the Richardson equations when there are three parties to the conflict (Richardson, 1960a), whose respective state variables are a, b and c:

$$\dot{a}_t = k_a(\hat{a} - a_t) + r_{ab}b_t + r_{ac}c_t \qquad (4.1a)$$

$$\dot{b}_t = k_b(\hat{b} - b_t) + r_{ba}a_t + r_{bc}c_t \qquad (4.1b)$$

$$\dot{c}_t = k_c(\hat{c} - c_t) + r_{ca}a_t + r_{cb}b_t \qquad (4.1c)$$

The first term on the right-hand sides of the above equations reflects a tendency for the state to return to an exogenous "normal" level, with the parameter $k_i > 0$ incorporating the speed at which this happens to actor i. The parameter r_{ij} denotes party i's *reaction coefficient* to party j's state. As is usual, we will drop time indices throughout the following discussion whenever we can do so without ambiguity.

In Richardson (1919)'s original account, the state variables represent the levels of armament of state actors involved in an arms race. The reaction coefficients r_{ij} are all positive as higher levels of armament on the part of other governments induce additional military procurement, *ceteris paribus*.

The computation of a stationary point for the above system is straightforward and leads to simple but clumsy expression, which we will not display here. The Jacobian for the system is

$$J = \begin{pmatrix} -k_a & r_{ab} & r_{ac} \\ r_{ba} & -k_b & r_{bc} \\ r_{ca} & r_{cb} & -k_c \end{pmatrix}$$

with the characteristic equation

$$\lambda^3 + (k_a + k_b + k_c)\lambda^2 + (k_ak_b + k_ak_c + k_bk_c - r_{ab}r_{ba} - r_{ac}r_{ca} - r_{bc}r_{cb})\lambda + \gamma = 0$$

where

$$\gamma = k_ak_bk_c - k_cr_{ab}r_{ba} - k_br_{ac}r_{ca} - k_ar_{bc}r_{cb} - r_{ac}r_{ba}r_{cb}$$

It is a tedious exercise to solve this for the eigenvalues of J. The equation has three solutions, one of which is real and two of which are complex. The signs of the real parts can be both positive and negative depending on the parameters of the system, in particular on the relative sizes of the k's and r's. As in the two-dimensional case, we find a stable node when $k > r$ and an unstable node otherwise.

B. First extension: negative parameters

Our first extension of this original Richardson model is based on the idea of admitting *negative* parameters r_{ij}. This leads to two interesting configurations detailed below. But note that these extensions are only possible if there are three or more parties to the conflict – the concentration on the two-agent case hitherto obscured this.

I. Attenuating agents

Let agent c be an "attenuator", which we define as a player whose activities *reduce* the armament / escalation level of both other parties to the conflict. An example (hopefully) would be NATO engaged in a peace keeping mission (Goldstein and Pevehouse, 1999). The state variable c can now be interpreted as an *involvement level*, which depends positively on the level of armament / aggression by the other parties, i.e. $r_{ca}, r_{cb} > 0$. However, $r_{ic} < 0$ for all $i \in (a, b)$.

Admitting negative values for some parameters opens up several new possibilities. For example, the following vector plot shows the case where $k_i = \frac{1}{20} \forall i$ and $|r_{ij}| = \frac{1}{10}$, but c's influence on the other two players is attenuating. This leads to the emergence of a *center* with cyclical trajectories and periodic motion of the armament levels, which has not so far been described in the literature on Richardson-type models. See the left panel in figure 4.1 on page 31.

Stable nodes also can display more complex dynamic behaviour than in the two-party case. For example, in the special case where $k_a = k_b = k_c$ and $r_{ca} = r_{cb} = 0.2$ while $r_{ab} = 0.3$, $r_{ba} = 0.1$ as well as $r_{ac} = r_{bc} = -0.2$, the numerical eigenvalues (up to three digits' precision) are $\lambda_1 = -0.688$, $\lambda_2 = -0.406 + 0.276i$ and $\lambda_3 = -0.406 - 0.276i$. The resulting asymmetric trajectories are illustrated in the vector plot in the left panel of figure 4.1 on page 31.

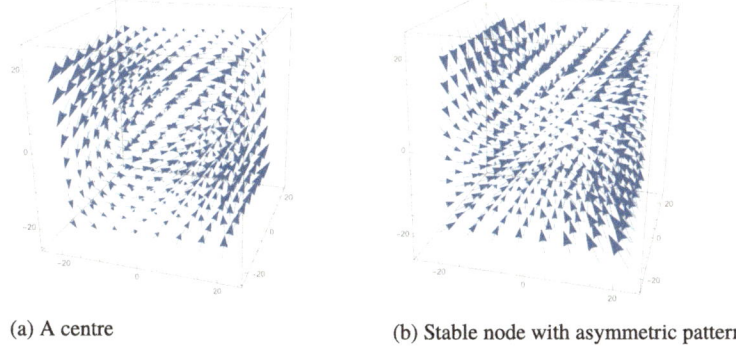

(a) A centre   (b) Stable node with asymmetric patterns

Figure 4.1: Additional dynamic patterns in the presence of attenuating agents

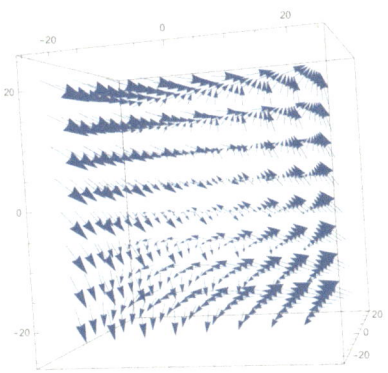

Figure 4.2: An unstable vortex in the presence of alliances

II.   Alliances

In an alliance, higher armament by one of the parties will lead – all other things being equal – to a reduction of effort by the other due to the familiar incentive to free-ride on the contribution of others (Sandler, 2004). That is, if a and b are allies in an otherwise standard conflict with c, we would expect $r_{ab}, r_{ba} < 0$, while all other coefficients remain positive.

Numerical experimentation using our standard example (where the $k_i =$ 0.05 and $|r_{ij}| = 0.1$) reveals that the system may now behave as an unstable vortex, with three imaginary eigenvalues, two of which have negative real parts. Figure 4.2 on page 31 below shows this particular example.

C. Second extension: a psychological reformulation of the Richardson equations

Boulding (1962) offered a *psychological* story to tell with the Richardson equations. In his version, the state variables measure the *hostility* of one party towards the other – in video game parlance, their "aggro levels". There is a tendency for the hostility level to regress to a base value $\hat{a}, \hat{b}$, and one party will escalate when their adversary's hostility towards them increases. This appears to be a natural interpretation of the equations in the two-agent case. But consider the system (4.1) in matrix form (we assume $\hat{a} = \hat{b} = \hat{c}$ for simplicity):

$$\begin{pmatrix} \dot{a} \\ \dot{b} \\ \dot{c} \end{pmatrix} = \begin{pmatrix} -k_a & r_{ab} & r_{ac} \\ r_{ba} & -k_b & r_{bc} \\ r_{ca} & r_{cb} & -k_c \end{pmatrix} \begin{pmatrix} a \\ b \\ c \end{pmatrix} \tag{4.2}$$

This equation shows that the Richardson equations *force an agent's hostility towards the other two to be the same*. There is also a nonnegativity restriction on the state variables which makes perfect sense when modelling arms races – where negative force levels are an impossibility –, but seems unsatisfactory in international relations, where there may exist sympathy, and where enmity can transmogrify into friendship (at least if you subscribe to idealism).

We now propose an extension of the model that removes these drawbacks. In doing so, we combine three ideas developed in the preceding sections:

1. Agents' attitudes towards other agents may differ, and they may be negative (friendship).
2. The nonnegativity restriction is dropped on all parameters except the one reflecting the rate of reversion to the "natural" aggressiveness level. This allows for attenuating agents as well as for alliances (see sub-sections I. and II.).
3. The interaction effect is taken to depend on the *escalation* of aggression experienced by an agent rather than its level (see sub-section B.).

The state of the system is now represented by a *two-dimensional matrix S* of size $n \times n$ rather than a vector, where n denotes both the number and the set of agents. Each element s_{ij} of S measures agent i's hostility towards j. The case where $i = j$ is considered as a general level of hostility of agent i which is not directed towards another agent in particular (and treated differently). We impose no *a priori* restrictions on s_{ij} as we want to permit empathy as well as hostility (where a negative s refers to the former in line with Goldstein (1992) scoring). It follows that the matrix of changes will also be of dimension $n \times n$.

The second building block of the model is a $n \times n \times n$ matrix $\mathcal{A}$ of parameters capturing the responsiveness to others' aggression levels. Each element a_{ijk} of $\mathcal{A}$ represents the change in agent i's attitude towards agent j as a result of agent k's hostility level. Under the proviso that we are limiting ourselves to exponential processes (linear changes in time), this framework is the most general one. The n^2 equations of motion in this system are the following:

$$\dot{s}_{ij} = a_{iji} (\hat{s}_i - s_{ii}) + \sum_{k \neq i}^{n} a_{ijk} s_{ki} \quad \forall \quad i, j \in n \qquad (4.3)$$

Equation (4.3) – with $a_{iji} > 0$ – reflects the standard property of the Richardson model that there exists a "natural" level of aggression $\hat{s}_i$ for each country i to which it would revert in the absence of any interaction between countries. It also captures these interactions, stipulating that country i's hostility (or empathy) towards country j changes as a result of the change in the hostility *other* countries exhibit towards i, where there is a k-specific linear effect.

D. Monte-Carlo simulations

Our extended version of the Richardson model presented in section C. above is very hard to solve analytically, particularly so because its Jacobian is three-dimensional. We therefore resort to numerical experimentation, using the Wolfram Language[1] script shown in the appendix on page 57.

The procedure basically allows the user to input a number of trials and iterations. For each trial, the parameter matrix $\mathcal{A}$ and the vector of natural aggression levels $\hat{a}_i$ are filled using a pseudo-random number generator. The user can specify the boundaries for this number generation, and the software ensures that all a_{iii} are non-negative according to the idea behind equation (4.3). S always starts filled with zeroes, but is then updated according to equation (4.3) for the specified number of iterations. We consider the system to *pseudo-converge* if the sum of all elements in S is lower than some hard-coded value, in our case one tenth of a thousand.

The overall simulation results are interesting. Figure 4.3 displays selected results for a typical Monte Carlo run with 100 trials using the hard coded parameters from the appendix, plotting the general hostility levels s_{ii} over time. Pseudo-convergence occurs in a minority of cases – 13 % in the example

---

1 For information regarding this computer language, refer to https://www.wolfram.com/language/.

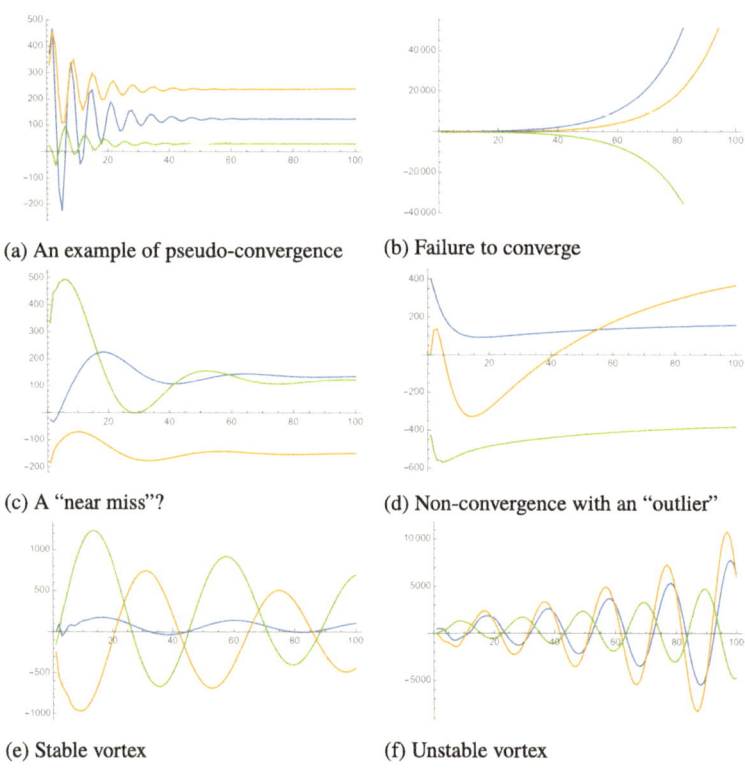

(a) An example of pseudo-convergence

(b) Failure to converge

(c) A "near miss"?

(d) Non-convergence with an "outlier"

(e) Stable vortex

(f) Unstable vortex

Figure 4.3: Typical results for simulation trials

run that figure 4.3 draws upon –, but it is by no means negligible. The number of repetitions mainly seems to be sufficient for the distincion between unstable and stable scenarios, with the possible exception of situations like the ones in panels (4.3c) and (4.3e).

Consistent with our argument about additional dynamic patterns arising in an incrementalist version of the Richardson equations (sub-section B. above), we find several typical patterns of conflict dynamics. Oscillations are a frequent occurence in both stable and unstable simulation trials, but instability is often characterised by monotonic "explosions" like the ones in panels (4.3b) and (4.3d) rather than increasing amplitude as in (4.3f).

Chapter 5: Empirical analysis

In this chapter, we present two empirical sketches to verify the theory developed in the preceding chapters of this book. We begin by looking at the 1998-2000 war between Eritreia and Ethiopia (section A.). This particular case study was chosen for three reasons:

1. A case can be made that this is a rare example of a two-party shooting war in which other actors played a minor role.
2. The war was fought using manoeuvre warfare by mechanised troops using late Soviet-era equipment, and so may be of particular interest to the contemporary student of war.
3. The region is the subject matter of NATO's "Crisis in East Cerasia" operational training scenario, for which free and unclassified material is available (see https://www.mscoe.org/content/uploads/2017/03/9-EXERCISE_SCENARIO.pdf, last checked on Dec 16th, 2020).

After a short description of the case study, we use both time series analysis techniques and structural equations modelling to analyse GDELT data for this conflict.

The second application (see section B.) builds on work by Francisco (2009), who uses a political science data set measuring protester turnout and the number of police forces engaged during demonstrations in various countries. While Francisco (2009) estimated a Lotka-Volterra model with these data, we extend this to the full general model introduced in chapter 2.

A.   The ERI-ETI war as case study for the two-agent Richardson model?

In order to provide an empirical illustration for the suitability of the model for two parties, two obvious prerequisites need to be met: first, one has to find a well-documented conflict in history with just two parties to it, and second, the state variables of the model need to be identified in the appertaining dataset.[1]

---

[1] We recognise in passing that Richardson (1960b) also played a pioneering role in the systematic collection of data about conflicts.

Regarding the first issue, we focus on the war between Ethiopia and Eritreia (hostilities lasted from May 1998 to May 2000,[2] but our dataset includes the three years preceding the outbreak of hostilities and following the ceasefire), arguing that this is indeed a conflict in which external players and mediators did not play a decisive role.

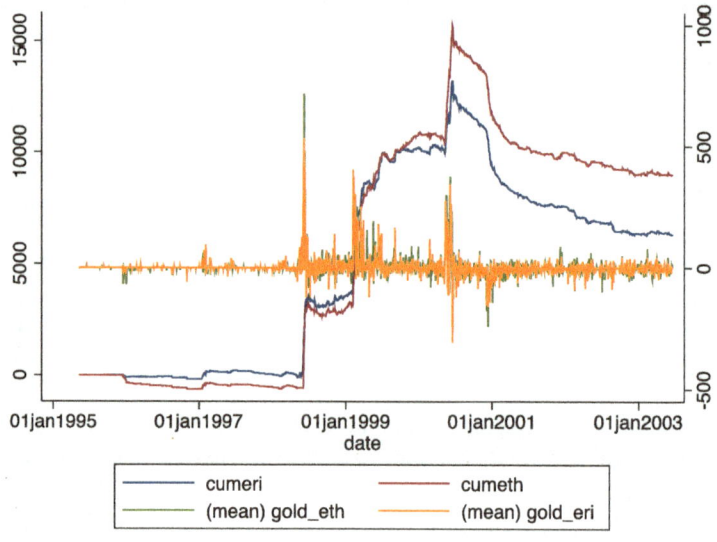

Figure 5.1: (Cumulative) Goldstein (1992) scores for the ETI-ERI war

I. Description of the data set

As to the second, we follow a large strand of literature using the GDELT[3] database of coded discrete event data (Goldstein and Pevehouse, 1999) . Our measure of (de-) *escalation* or the *change of aggressiveness* is the Goldstein score (Goldstein, 1992), which assigns each conflictary (and cooperative) action an integer in the interval $[-10; 10]$ indicating the flow impact on relations between the involved parties.

---

2 See https://en.wikipedia.org/wiki/Eritrean-Ethiopian_War, last checked on Dec 16th, 2020.

3 The GDELT Project – Global Database of Events, Language and Tone – http: //gdeltproject.org/, last checked on Dec 16th, 2020.

In a first attempt to implement the Richardson equations econometrically, it is tempting to interpret the model literally and to use the sum of the (undiscounted) Goldstein scores accumulated over the course of the conflict as our state variables. (This obviously requires us to fix the starting values for the state variables $a(0)$, $b(0)$ at some arbitrary level – zero in the following illustration.) Figure 5.1 plots the four resulting time series over time.[4]

On inspection of figure 5.1, we observe that the accumulated Goldstein scores remained constant in the years preceding the war, and that they abated in the aftermath of the ceasefire. We also find the expected steep increase during hostilities. The change of aggressiveness during the war is dominated by three extreme peaks corresponding to major campaigns[5] and also influenced by the onset of the rain season, which impeded the movement of motorised troops. These are obviously exogenous shocks not explained by the standard Richardson model.

II.   Time series analysis and the suitability of the accumulated Goldstein score

Let us begin by analysing the time series more closely. We immediately find descriptive evidence suggestive of differences between phases of the conflict. In particular, by looking at the correlograms of the Goldstein score time series separately for the war and the three years leading up to it (figure 5.2), we see that the shooting war differs from the other two phases of this conflict.

Not only does there seem to be more autocorrelation during the war, but significant lags appear to be clustered over the first week. This is suggestive of the effect of *military planning leading to continuous activity*. During the crisis before the war, on the other hand, significant lags were not concentrated in the same manner, and the correlation coefficients do not shrink over time as they do during the war.

Table 5.1 on page 41 summarises the results of a formal time series analysis of our data set. An augmented Dickey-Fuller test using 21 lags as suggested by the Schwert criterion allows us to reject the null of a unit root for our time series of Goldstein scores (analysing the pre-war, wartime and post-war periods separately). Unsurprisingly, this is not the case for the state

---

4   The two flow variables are called "eri" – the sum of the Goldstein indices assigned to Eritreia's actions towards Ethiopia on a given day – and "eth", while we refer to the stock variables as "cumeri" and "cumeth".

5   The Eritrean attack on Badme in May 1998 including the subsequent air war, Ethiopia's offensive of February 1999, and the final Ethiopian attack in May 2000 that severed Eritreian lines of communication and paved the way for the ceasefire.

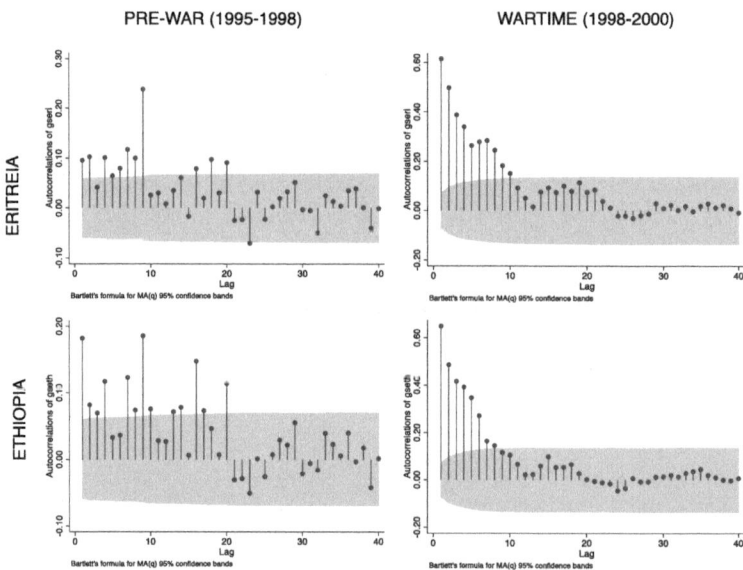

Figure 5.2: Correlograms for our time series of Goldstein scores

variable. We use a Johansen test for cointegration – again with 21 lags – and find that the time series for the Goldstein scores are clearly cointegrated at all conventional levels of significance, while no significant evidence of cointegration can be found for the accumulated scores with the interesting exception of the post-war period.

Table 5.1 reveals major problems with our tentative attempt to implement the Richardson model by using accumulated, undiscounted Goldstein scores as state variables. Most importantly, a conflict party's accumulated Goldstein scores *do not Granger cause* their daily escalation. This, however, is a clear implication of the Richardson approach as this stipulates a reversion to the "natural" aggression levels $\hat{a}, \hat{b}$.[6]

---

6 Interestingly, we do see a causality running from the cumulated Goldstein scores to the escalation *by the other party*, which is consistent with the Richardson story.

Table 5.1: Summary of time series analyses

Type of analysis	Time series	1995-1998	1998-2000	2000-2003
Stationarity	eth	yes***	yes***	yes***
	eri	yes***	yes***	yes***
	cumeth	no	no	no
	cumeri	no	no	no
Cointegration	eri, eth	yes***	yes***	yes***
	cumeri, cumeth	no	no	yes***
Granger causality	eri ⇒ eth	yes***	yes***	yes***
	eth ⇒ eri	yes***	yes***	yes***
	cumeth ⇒ eri	yes***	yes***	yes***
	cumeri ⇒ eth	yes***	yes***	yes***
	cumeth ⇒ eth	no	no	no
	cumeri ⇒ eri	no	no	no

III. Structural model estimations

For this reason, discard the cumeri and cumeth variables and turn to the estimation strategy expounded by Francisco (2009). This author regresses *present* current aggression levels for two parties on lagged values of the same variables, using a Lotka-Volterra specification (i.e., forcing the coefficient on the other party's state to be zero). As this would contradict our preliminary findings that show some (non-interacted) reaction of the parties to their counterpart's aggression, we propose to estimate a *general* model which includes all possible terms from the Lanchester, Lotka-Volterra, and Richardson specifications:

$$eri_t = a_0 + a_1 eri_{t-1} + a_2 eti_{t-1} + a_3 eri_{t-1} eti_{t-1} \qquad (5.1)$$

$$eti_t = b_0 + b_1 eti_{t-1} + b_2 eri_{t-1} + b_3 eti_{t-1} eri_{t-1} \qquad (5.2)$$

We are aware that this means taking a rather explorative attitude. We believe, however, that such an attitude is justified by our final goal of identifying patterns of conflict dynamics. We allow for the errors between the variables on the LHS to be correlated as they are endogenous, and levels of significance are based on robust standard errors. Table 5.2 below summarises our estimation results for the periods preceding the war, the shooting war itself, and the aftermath.

The three periods are clearly not alike, with the years leading up to the war appearing the most chaotic. For the war itself, however, we get results that are broadly consistent with the Richardson approach. The highly significant

41

Table 5.2: Summary of SEM analyses

	1995-1998	1998-2000	2000-2003
a_0	-0.0429	4.890 ***	-4.15 ***
a_1	0.0451	0.5620 ***	0.1224 *
a_2	0.0704 *	0.1388 (?)	0.0682
a_3	0.0001	-0.0002	-0.0011 *
b_0	-0.3944 **	6.300 ***	-3.618 ***
b_1	0.2198	0.3456 ***	0.1243 **
b_2	-0.0533	0.3309 **	0.0454
b_3	-0.0001	0.0004	-0.0021 ***

parameters a_1 and b_1 are both smaller than one, which we would expect in a Richardson model given that we regress present states on their lagged values. Both the reaction effects are positive and b_2 is also significant. Its counterpart $_2$ barely escapes being significant at the 10 % level.

The estimates for the post-war period, on the other hand, do not sit well with the Richardson model. In particular, the coefficient of direct reaction (b_3) loses significance, and there are now significant interaction effects. As the signs on the own and the interaction effect remain consistent, however, this pattern is incompatible with the Lotka-Volterra approach and more in line with a linear Lanchester law augmented by rapid adaptation to a (lower) target level of aggression.

B. Re-estimating the Francisco (2009) data

We build on the work done and data collected by Francisco (2009). This author uses a bespoke data collected at his institution and supported by the National Science Foundation (Francisco, 2009, vii).[7]

For the period from 1980 to 1995, we construct daily time series of the number of state agents employed in counter-riot activities ("state"), the number of protesters engaged in demonstrations ("protesters") als well as the numbers of casualties on both sides (both fatal and non-fatal). We will refrain from exploiting the latter variables in this monograph as our objective here is to demonstrate the method rather than present material results. For the same reason, we only consider three countries: Germany (FRG), France (FRA) and Spain (ESP).

---

7 We downloaded the data from the project's web site at http://web.ku.edu/, last checked on Dec 16th, 2020.

We use the same structural equation model as in sub-section III. above. Figure 5.3 on page 43 shows its graphical representation in the STATA model builder.[8]

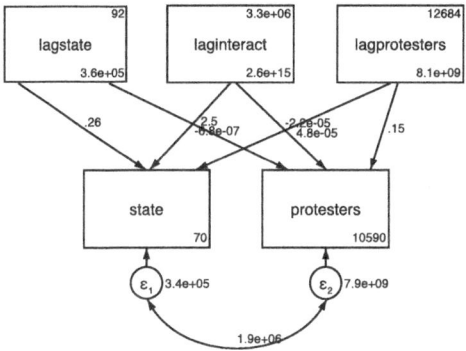

Figure 5.3: Graphical representation of SEM model

The table on page 44 summarises the results of our estimation for three countries – France, Germany, and Spain – and the 1980-95 period. We also run separate country-specific models for the first and last thirds of this period, respectively.

To begin with, note that the significance of the results in some cases depends on the "normal" standard errors, which makes some of our results dubious. With that caveat in mind, a couple of observations can be made:

1. Countries seem to differ. In particular, Spain not only exhibits a somewhat different pattern of significant effects, but also differs in its (negative) sign on the reaction parameter for the protesters. The obvious interpretation is that police presence acted as a deterrent to protesters in Spain while having hardly any significance in Germany and France.
2. We also find an indication that some change in the dynamics of conflict occurred between the first and the last third of our observation period.

---

8 STATA is commercial statistical software supplied by STATA Corp (https://www.stata. com/company/, last checked on Dec 16th, 2020). For a course on implementing SEM models in Stata see Acock (2013) und Ramlall (2016).

Table 5.3: Re-estimating the Francesco (2009) dataset using a general model

Country	Time	S.E.	d(protest)			d(police)		
			own	reaction	inter	own	reaction	inter
FRA	80-95	std	0.282 ***	3.541	-0.293E-4	0.170 ***	0.553E-4	-1,45E-7 ***
	80-95	robust	0.282 ***	3.541	-0.293E-4	0.170 **	0.553E-4 *	-1.45E-7
	80-85	std	0.175 ***	1.597	-0.192E-4	0.415 ***	-0.192E-4	-3.11E-7 ***
	80-85	robust	0.175 *	1.597	-0.192E-4	0.415 ***	-0.192E-4	-3.11E-7 ***
	90-95	std	0.303 ***	0.003	0.349E-4	0.070 ***	0.174E-4	-1,45E-7
	90-95	robust	0.303 **	0.003	-0.349E-4	0.070	0.174E-4	-1,45E-7
DEU	80-95	std	0.152 ***	2.524	-0.22E-4	0.262 ***	0.482E-4	-6.75E-7
	80-95	robust	0.152 ***	2.524	-0.22E-4	0.262 ***	0.482E-4	-6.75E-7
	80-85	std	0.221 ***	6.896 *	-0.952E-4 *	0.265 ***	0.804E-4	-1.70E-6
	80-85	robust	0.221 **	6.896	-0.952E-4	0.265	0.804E-4	-1.70E-6
	90-95	std	0.088 ***	1.088	-0.307E-4	0.400 ***	0.00013**	-9.99E-7 ***
	90-95	robust	0.088 **	1.088	-0.307E-4	0.400 ***	0.00013 **	-9.99E-7 **
ESP	80-95	std	0.195 ***	-4.63E-6 *	12.775	0.0560	5.79E-7	-1.41E-8
	80-95	robust	0.195	-4.63E-6 *	12.775	0.0560	5.79E-7	-1.41E-8
	80-85	std	0.0629 **	-0.284E-4	20.56 **	0.151 ***	0.00016 *	-4.08E-7 ***
	80-85	robust	0.0629 **	-0.284E-4	20.56 **	0.151 ***	0.00016 *	-4.08E-7 ***
	90-95	std	0.397 ***	-10.59	-3.02E-7	0.021	-0.999E-4	-4.56E-9
	90-95	robust	0.397	-10.59	-3.02E-7	0.021	-0.999E-4	-4.56E-9

For France, we have significant positive own and negative interaction effects for the first half of the 1980, and cannot find any interaction effct for the early 1990s. Germany has no robust effects (except a dependence of the number of protesters) for the early 1980s, while we find police behaviour to depend on all three parameters in a significant manner.
3. We consistently find positive – and, to the most part – significant own effects. This should not come as a surprise as planning of operations leads to autocorrelation (see figure 5.2 on page 40 above).

Failure to find significant positive reaction effects implies that the conflict at hand is *not driven by a standard Boulding-Richardson mechanism*. The co-existence of a significant own and interaction effect appears consistent with a Lotka-Volterra model, except that in this case the respective parameters for the two parties should exhibit opposite signs, which they do not.

The data seem most consistent with *Lanchester's linear model* augmented by a growth component that captures autocorrelation (the persistence of operations over several days).

All in all, these are rather weak and mixed results. We find that an application of the linear conflict model to real data can detect some patterns, but clearly more work on empirical specifications and methods is needed to bolster up this line of research.

Chapter 6: Bounded rationality in dynamic models

The central weakness of the linear conflict models expounded in this little volume is that agents' decisions are not derived from optimising calculations. This is precisely why this type of model appears to have been left at the wayside of economic efforts to model conflict. On the other hand, we need to keep in mind the technical difficulties arising from the use of game theory as an analytical tool in a dynamic context (Beckmann and Reimer, 2014).

For when elements of control theory are integrated into a classical non-cooperative game, we obtain a *differential game* (Isaacs, 1954). These models are of high interest, but fraught with two problems: first, the resulting systems of differential equations frequently do not afford an analytical solution, in particular if the equations of motion contain nonlinearities. Second, the calculations involved are so complex that it is hardly credible that real-world decision-makers would employ them at all. In the absence of repetition and learning, which is typical of armed conflict scenarios, it is difficult to rationalise how agents could "feel their way" towards equilibrium.[1]

We therefore conclude the present monograph by suggesting a boundedly rational heuristic for deciding in a differential game. This heuristic was used in Frey and Rohner (2007) as well as in Beckmann and Reimer (2014), but has not to our knowledge been analysed as a general decision rule. This heuristic also avoids the infinite utility problems that would ensue in an infinitely repeated game with no discounting.

A. Basic approach

Consider a game with two agents $i \in \{1, 2\}$, each of whom has a compact set of pure strategies S_i. Denote strategy choices by σ_i and payoffs by $\pi_i(\sigma_i, \sigma_j)$ where j is the "other" player. The first order condition for an optimal choice given $\overline{\sigma}_2$ is the obvious

$$\frac{\partial \pi(\sigma_i, \sigma_j)}{\partial \sigma_i} = 0 \qquad (6.1)$$

---

1 Applications where optimal solutions are sought in order to program them into a computer, as in the pursuit-evasion models Isaacs (1965), are a different matter altogether.

From the above, one can compute player i's reaction function by solving for σ_i and then find the Nash equilibrium (NE) as the solution of the system of the two reaction functions.

We now consider a simple dynamic version of the above game: strategy choices are made over a (possibly endless) interval of time $t \in [0; T]$. At each point in time, an identical version of the stage game is played; that is, the state of the system does not change as a consequence of agents' choices (an assumption we will relax in the next section). Let us use this simple scenario to posit a simple heuristic and explore its properties.

I. The decision heuristic

At time t, agent i takes j's current strategy σ_j as given (as in the Nash conjecture) and as time invariant — that is, agents are assumed to be *myopic*. We then assume the agent to calculate the optimal *static* response according to equation (6.1) and close a proportion α_i of the gap between this myopic optimum and its current strategy $\sigma_i(t)$. The equation of motion for i's control is given by

$$\dot{\sigma}_i = \alpha_i \left(\mathrm{argmax}(\pi_i(\sigma_i(t), \sigma_j(t))) - \sigma_i(t) \right) \tag{6.2}$$

In addition to being myopic, this heuristic has two important properties:

1. Choices have a *history*, in particular, there is an exogenous starting strategy $\sigma(0)$. This can reflect such things as initial readiness or deployment in a theory of conflict.

2. Agents can differ in their *speed of adaptation* to the current myopic optimum. This property can be used to model differing speeds of decision-making processes or different flexibilities in implementing policy changes.

II. Convergence to Nash equilibrium

Denote i's the reaction function as $\sigma_i^* = \sigma_i^*(\sigma_j(t))$. Equation (6.2) can then be rewritten as

$$\dot{\sigma}_i = \alpha_i \left(\sigma_i^*(\sigma_j(t)) - \sigma_i(t) \right) \tag{6.3}$$

From total differentiation of i's first-order condition, we obtain

$$\frac{\partial \sigma_i^*}{\partial \sigma_j} = -\frac{\frac{\partial^2 \pi_i}{\partial \sigma_i \partial \sigma_j}}{\frac{\partial^2 \pi_i}{\partial \sigma_i^2}} = -\frac{d_{ij}}{d_{ii}} \qquad (6.4)$$

We write d_{ij} as a shorthand for $\frac{\partial^2 \pi_i}{\partial \sigma_i \partial \sigma_j}$. Obviously, from the second order conditions for a maximum, we have $d_{11} < 0$ and $d_{22} < 0$, and the sign of the mixed partials depends on whether there is strategic complementarity or substitutability. Using (6.4), the Jacobian of our system is

$$J = \begin{pmatrix} -\alpha_1 & -\alpha_1 \frac{d_{12}}{d_{11}} \\ -\alpha_2 \frac{d_{21}}{d_{22}} & -\alpha_2 \end{pmatrix}$$

The eigenvalues of this Jacobian are given by

$$e_{1,2} = -\frac{1}{2}\left(\alpha_1 + \alpha_2 \pm \sqrt{\frac{4\alpha_1\alpha_2 d_{12}d_{21} + (\alpha_1 - \alpha_2)^2 d_{11}d_{22}}{d_{11}d_{22}}} \right)$$

Note that the reaction speeds α_i are non-negative. If the mixed partials have the same sign – i.e., if the game is weakly symmetric in the sense that the complementarity or otherwise of strategies is the same for both players –, then the eigenvalues will both be real-valued and no oscillations can occur. If the reaction speeds are identical, then the usual "mixed partial rule" $0 < d_{12}d_{21} < d_{11}d_{22}$ is a sufficient stability condition as it ensures that both eigenvalues will be real-valued and negative.

B. Differential games

I. The state equation

The typical differential game model differs from the above game in that the players' *instantaneous utility* or payoff depends on the current value $x(t)$ of a *state variable* — or a vector of such variables —, while the change of the system state is a function of the system's history and the players' strategies or *controls*. Formally we have

$$\pi_i(t) = \pi_i(x(t)) \qquad (6.5)$$

$$\dot{x} = f(x(t), \sigma_1(t), \sigma_2(t)) \qquad (6.6)$$

We can translate this into the format of equation (6.1) by integration. Notice that

$$x(t) = \int_0^t f(x(t), \sigma_1(t), \sigma_2(t)) \mathrm{d}t$$

to find

$$\pi_i(x_0, \sigma_1, \sigma_2) = \pi(\int_0^t f(x(t), \sigma_1(t), \sigma_2(t)) \mathrm{d}t)$$

Agent i's payoff at time t is therefore a function both of the history of play and of the initial condition of the system x_0. We can still apply the heuristic represented by equation (6.2): players are assumed to treat the current state of the system $x(t)$ and their opponents' current strategies as given, calculate their optimal response in this static setting and then close a percentage α between the "best" response and their current strategy σ_i. The difference between the differential game and the repeated static game of the previous section is that the desired end state is now a moving target — the process no longer converges to the NE of the stage game, but to the NE of a static game described by *the system's state at termination $x(T)$*. (If time is infinite, the target can continue moving indefinitely.)

II. First example: the political business cycle

We now consider a simple application of our approach: the classical political business cycle model (Drazen 2000). There are two players, the government and the private sector. Let the short-run trade-off between unemployment $u(t)$ and inflation $p(t)$ be given by the simple Phillips curve

$$u(t) = \theta - (p(t) - p^E(t)) \tag{6.7}$$

where p represents the actual rate of inflation — the government's control — and p^E is the expected rate of inflation, controlled by the private sector. The government is assumed to minimise a quadratic loss function defined over the two bads inflation and unemployment:

$$w(t) = p(t)^2 + \kappa u(t)^2 \tag{6.8}$$

where κ is an exogenous weight increasing in the government's leftiness. As in the literature, we assume that the private sector's goal is to minimise the squared forecast error $(p(t) - p^E(t))^2$. The usual specification of adaptive expectations can be dropped because it is built into our behavioural assumptions as long as $\alpha < 1$.

As for the private sector, its optimal choice at each point of time (given a static reference) is obvious: it is to set $p^E(t) = p(t)$. However, only a proportion α of this gap can be closed. This yields the equation of motion

$$\dot{p}^E = \alpha(p(t) - p^E(t))$$

As for the government, we plug equation (6.7) into equation (6.8) to get

$$w(t) = (1 + \kappa)p(t)^2 - 2\kappa p(t)(p^E + \theta) + \kappa p^{E2} + 2\kappa p^E\theta + \kappa\theta^2$$

The myopically optimal response is therefore

$$p(t) = \frac{\kappa}{1 + \kappa}(p^E(t) + \theta)$$

which yields the following equation of motion (assuming for simplicity that the αs are the same):

$$\dot{p} = \alpha\left(\frac{\kappa}{1 + \kappa}(p^E(t) + \theta) - p(t)\right)$$

These equations of motion can be studied in the usual way. First, we let $\dot{p}^E = \dot{p} = 0$ to find the steady state $p^{E*} = p^* = \kappa\theta$. We then compute the eigenvalues of the Jabobian

$$J = \begin{pmatrix} -\alpha & \alpha \\ \frac{\kappa\alpha}{1+\kappa} & -\alpha \end{pmatrix}$$

to find $e_{1,2} = -\frac{\alpha}{1+\kappa}\left(1 + \alpha \pm \sqrt{\kappa + \kappa^2}\right)$, both of which are real-valued and at least one of which is negative. The steady state will therefore be either stable or saddle point stable (if the signs differ).

III. Second example: a dynamic rent-seeking model

The second example extends the well-known basic model of rent-seeking (or, alternatively, wasteful military conflict) to a dynamic setting (Rowley, Tollison and Tullock 2013). Assume we have two agents vying for resources. At every point of time, agent i has $r_i(t)$ units of the resource pool under her control, which she can either invest into some productive activity or spend on fighting f. Denote the constant rate of return for peaceful production $\rho > 1$. The pool of resources that is up for grabs at time t is then $\rho \sum_j(r_j - f_j)$, and we assume that agent i receives a share p_i according to a standard *contest success function* (Hirshleifer 2001) $p_i = \frac{f_i}{\sum_j f_j}$. The equation of motion for i's resources is therefore

$$\dot{r}_i = \frac{f_i}{\sum_j f_j} \rho \sum_j (r_j - f_j) - r_i \qquad (6.9)$$

In our bounded rationality model, agent i will choose f_i in such a way as to maximise this net gain of resources. The first-order condition for this problem simplifies to:

$$f_i \sum_j (r_j - f_j) + (\sum_j (r_j - f_j) - f_i) \sum_j f_j = 0 \qquad (6.10)$$

For the remainder of this example, let us focus on the two-agent case. Using (6.10), we find that both agents aspire to realise $f_{1,2} = \frac{3}{8}(r_1 + r_2)$. We therefore have the following equations of motion for the controls:

$$\dot{f}_i = \alpha_i \left(\frac{3}{8}(r_1 + r_2) - f_i \right) \qquad (6.11)$$

As the state and control variables differ in this model, the dynamics of the model come from a system of four ordinary differential equations – (6.9) and (6.11) –, half of which are non-linear. The nonlinearities lead to the usual kind of problems when attempting to solve the system explicitly.

In order to solve the equation system for a steady state, observe that we must have $f_1, f_2 \neq 0$ due to (6.9). From (6.11), we conclude that the r_is must also be nonzero. We proceed to prove the nonexistence of a steady state in three steps.

1. Consider a symmetric steady state with $f_1 = f_2 = f > 0$. We can then subtract the two versions of (6.9) to find that $r_1 = r_2 = r$. Substitute into (6.11) to find $f = \frac{3}{4}r$. Plugging this into (6.9), we find $r(\rho - \frac{3}{8}\rho - 1) = 0$, which implies that either $r = 0$ – which would lead to a contradiction – or $\rho = \frac{1}{1-3/8}$ and r free.

2. In any solution, we can add the two equations (6.9) to find, after some rearranging, that $(\rho - 1)(r_1 + r_2) = \rho(f_1 + f_2)$. Using (6.11), this in turn implies $(\rho - 1)(r_1 + r_2) = \rho\frac{3}{4}(r_1 + r_2)$ or $\rho = 4$.

3. Finally, our first (symmetric) version is a special case of the second, and so the second argument must apply to the first case also. However, ρ cannot simultaneously be equal to 4 and 1.6. Consequently, not steady state with nonzero values for r_i and f_i exists.

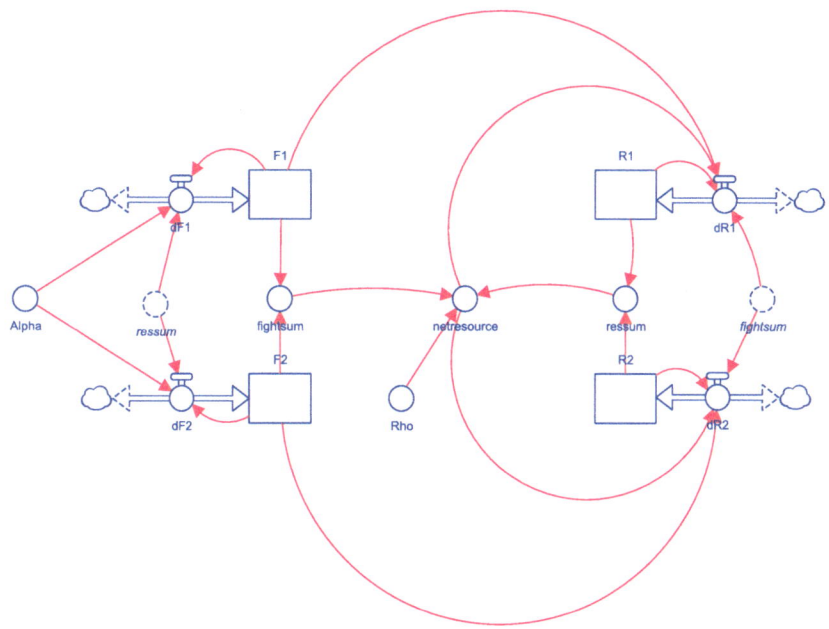

Figure 6.1: A *Stella* simulation of the dynamic rent-seeking model

This means that numerical techniques must be used to explore the properties of this model. Figure 6.1 below shows a simulation model of equations (6.9) and (6.11) set up using *Stella*.[2]

It is easy to explore this model and to find that the typical results are not very sensitive to one's choice of parameter values. Figure 6.2 displays agent 2's fighting effort over time when we set $f_1(0) = f_2(0) = 100$, $r_1(0) = r_2(0) = 1000$, $\rho = 1.1$ and $\alpha_{1,2} = \frac{3}{4}$. We see that fighting intensifies in the beginning as the parties try to acquire the existing resources, but then decreases again as resources are depleted. Production fails to keep up with resource use for fighting, and the typical PD-type inefficiencies of rent-seeking models are clearly evident. In our model, *all* resources will be used up in the end as the system asymptotically approaches the origin ($f_1 = f_2 = r_1 = r_2 = 0$).

---

2 See https://www.iseesystems.com, last checked on Dec 16th, 2020.

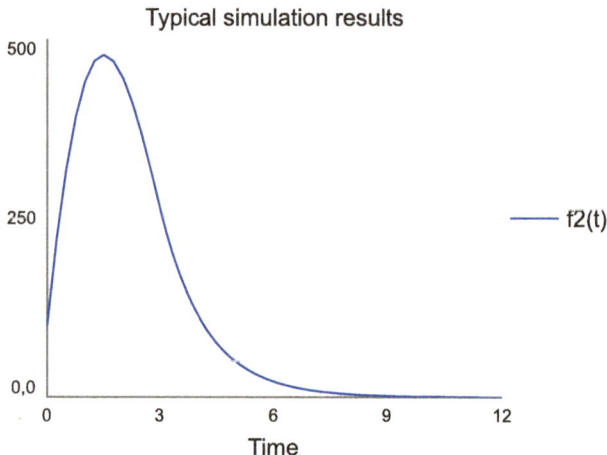

Figure 6.2: Results from a typical run of the simulation model

C. Comments

This concluding chapter has illustrated how a boundedly rational heuristic can be used to simplify differential games. The proposed decision rule is intuitively plausible and also simplifies both the calculations required of the agents and the resulting differential equations describing the behaviour of the system in such a way that analytical solutions can become available. Its basic assumptions resemble adaptive expectations as they were used in early dynamic models in the 1950s, and are admittedly rather simple. In contrast to these older models, however, they do contain an element of optimisation, and represent what we may consider the "other extreme" when compared to the highly complicated calculations involved in solving differential games (if that is at all possible in a technical sense). We suggest that approaches such as the present one can help to make some problems in combat modelling analytically tractable.

Chapter 7: Conclusion

Nicht was wir gedacht haben, halten wir für ein Verdienst um die Theorie, sondern die Art, wie wir es gedacht haben.
– Clausewitz, Vom Kriege, p. 361

The objective of this little monograph is to revisit *linear dynamic conflict models* in the Lanchester (1916) and Richardson (1919) traditions. The ulterior motive is to explore whether these models can fruitfully be used as the *basis for a taxonomy of conflict dynamics*. If that were the case, there ought to be systematic and significant differences between the parameters of the model when estimated for different (phases of) conflicts.

We began by discussing a simple linear differential equation model that includes Lanchester, Richardson and Lotka-Volterra equations (amongst others) as special cases. Four simple and easy to interpret building blocks were identified. The signs on the coefficients of these building blocks (and their magnitude) then determined (a) which sub-type of model applies, (b) whether the stationary points (if they exist) are stable and (c) which forms the time paths of the state variables can take. In theory, we can say that the coefficients describe the *pattern of conflict dynamics* that applies within the confines of the linear model.

As an example, the Richardson (1960a) equations were discussed at some length. This included an analysis of the stability properties of the standard model as well as an introduction of several extensions that might be of some independent interest. In particular, the three-party model with parameters describing the *psychological* reaction to other party's aggression allowed for the analysis of attenuators – such as UN peacekeepers – and alliances.

Returning to the basic model, we sketched a potential empirical application using structured equation modelling (SEM) and time series analysis techniques. Two case studies were considered in a rather explorative fashion. We did find some evidence of patterns in autocorrelation and some statistically significant differences in parameter signs between phases of conflict. However, the evidence appears mixed – in particular, we have not identified a systematic source for the differences between the various patterns discerned in the study.

We thus need to do more work. While the present monograph can serve as a proof of concept, substantive theory needs to be developed in order to derive *hypotheses* about the signs of the coefficients. This, however, is not a task for formal economic theorising and econometric analysis alone. It

55

requires an intradisciplinary effort that uses the formal model as its engine, but draws on political science and history for both inspiration and content. This is a typical task for a transdisciplinary research unit such as the GIDS, which can also provide a link to practitioners in the field.

Appendix : Programme listing

```
params = Array[a, {3, 3, 3}]
states = Array[x, {3, 3}]
changes = Array[y, {3, 3}]
naturals = Array[n, 3]
maxparam = 1
minparam = -1
maxturns = 100
attempts = 100
att = 1;
results1 = {};
results12 = {};
results13 = {};
results2 = {};
results3 = {};
nats = {};
pars = {};
stabruns = 0;
While[att <= attempts,
  (*Initialisierung des Runs*)
  For[i = 1, i < 4, i++,
   {n[i] = RandomReal[{-500, 500}],
    For[j = 1, j < 4, j++,
     {x[i, j] = RandomReal[{-500, 500}],
      y[i, j] = 0,
      For[k = 1, k < 4, k++,
       If[i == k,
        a[i, j, k] = RandomReal[{0, maxparam}],
        a[i, j, k] = RandomReal[{minparam, maxparam}]
        ]
       ]
      }
     ]
    }
   ];
  AppendTo[pars, params];
  AppendTo[nats, {n[1], n[2], n[3]}];
  (*Beginn des Runs*)

  (*Print["Parameter: ",params];
  Print["Naturals: ",naturals];*)
  turn = 1;
  successes = 0;
  (*Beginn der Timesteps*)
  While[turn <= maxturns,
   {sums = 0;
```

57

```
For[i = 1, i < 4, i++,
 {For[j = 1, j < 4, j++,
   {tempvar = 0,
    For[k = 1, k < 4, k++,
     If[i == k,
      tempvar = tempvar + a[i, j, k]*(n[i] - x[k, i]),
      tempvar = tempvar + a[i, j, k]*y[k, i]
     ]
    ],
    y[i, j] = tempvar, x[i, j] = x[i, j] + y[i, j]
   }
  ]
 }
];
AppendTo[results1, Part[Part[states, 1], 1]];
AppendTo[results2, Part[Part[states, 2], 2]];
AppendTo[results3, Part[Part[states, 3], 3]];
AppendTo[results12, Part[Part[states, 1], 2]];
AppendTo[results13, Part[Part[states, 1], 3]];
(*StabilitÃ¤tsprÃ¼fung*)
For[i = 1, i < 4, i++,
 For[j = 1, j < 4, j++,
  sums = sums + Abs[y[i, j]]
 ]];
(*StabilitÃ¤tskriterium*)

If[sums < 0.0001, {successes++;
  Print["Pseudo-StabilitÃ¤t in Run ", att, " zum Zeitpunkt ",
   turn]}]
 };
 turn++];
(*Print["Run: ",  att , ", Stabile Turns: ",  successes];*)
(*If[
successes>0,{stabruns++;Print["Pseudo-StabilitÃ¤t in Run ", att,
" zum Zeitpunkt ", turn]}];*)
 att++];
stabruns
(*ListPlot[results1];
ListPlot[results2];
ListPlot[results3];*)
```

Bibliography

Acock, A. C. (2013). *Discovering Structural Equation Modeling Using Stata* (2 ed.). Stata Press.

Anderton, C. H. and J. R. Carter (2009). *Principles of Conflict Economics.* Cambridge UP.

Atkinson, M. P., A. Gutfraind, and M. Kress (2012). When do armed revolts succeed: lessons from lanchester theory. *Journal of the Operational Research Society 63,* 1363–1373.

Baker, M. J. and E. H. Bulte (2005). Kings and vikings: on the dynamics of competitive agglomeration. Technical report, Department of Economics, Tilburg University.

Beckmann, K. B. and L. Reimer (2014). Dynamics of military conflict: an economics perspective. *Review of Economics 65,* 265–285.

Biddle, S. (2004). *Military Power.* Princeton and Oxford: Princeton UP.

Boulding, K. E. (1962). *Conflict and Defence: A General Theory.* New York: Harper Row.

Brams, S. J. (1994). *Theory of Moves.* Cambridge University Press.

Brams, S. J. (2011). *Game Theory and the Humanities.* MIT Press.

Bruns, B. (2010). Navigating the topology of 2x2 games: an intoductory note on payoff families, normalization, and natural order. Arxiv preprint arXiv:1010.4727.

Congleton, R. D., A. L. Hillman, and K. A. Konrad (Eds.) (2008). *40 Years of Research on Rent Seeking.* Berlin and Heidelberg: Springer.

Francisco, R. A. (2009). *Dynamics of Conflict.* Number ISBN-13: 978-1441925886. Springer.

Frey, B. S. and D. Rohner (2007). Blood and ink! the common-interest-game between terrorists and the media. *Public Choice 133,* 129–145.

Garfinkel, M. R. and S. Skaperdas (2007). Economics of conflict. In T. Sandler and K. Harley (Eds.), *Handbook of Defense Economics,* Volume 2, pp. 649–709. Elsevier.

Goldstein, J. S. (1992, June). A conflict-cooperation scale for weis events data. *The Journal of Conflict Resolution 36*(2), 369–385.

Goldstein, J. S. and J. Pevehouse (1999, August). Serbian compliance or defiance in kosovo? statistical analysis and real-time predictions. *The Journal of Conflict Resolution 43*(4), 538–546.

Hirshleifer, J. (2001). *The Dark Side of the Force.* Cambridge UP.

Hunt, J. (1995). Lewis fry richardson and his contributions to mathematics, meteorology, and models of conflict. *Annual Review of Fluid Mechanics 30: xiii- xxxvi.*

Intriligator, M. D. and D. L. Brito (1988). A predator-prey model of guerrilla warfare. *Synthese 76*(2), 235–244.

Intriligator, M. D. and D. L. Brito (1990). An economic model of guerrilla warfare. *International Interactions 15*(3-4).

Isaacs, R. (1954). Differential games. part i: Introduction. Technical report, RAND.

Isaacs, R. (1965). *Differential Games.* John Wiley & Sons, Inc.

Lanchester, F. W. (1916). *Aircraft in Warfare: The Dawn of the Fourth Arm.* New York: Appleton.

Lanchester, F. W. (1956). Mathematics in warfare. In J. Newman (Ed.), *The World of Mathematics,* pp. 2138–2157. New York: Simon and Schuster.

Lee, C.-T. (2007). A new explanation of arms races in the third world: a differential game model. *Journal of Economics and Management* 5(2), 161–176.

MacKay, N. J. (2006). Lanchester combat models. *Mathematics Today*.

Perlo-Freeman, S. (2006). The topology of conflict and co-operation. University of the West of England, Bristol.

Protopopescu, V., R. T. Santoro, J. Dockery, R. L. Cox, and J. M. Barnes (1987). Combat modeling with partial differential equations. Technical report, Oak Ridge National Laboratory.

Ramlall, I. (2016). *Applied Structural Equation Modelling for Researchers and Practitioners: Using R and Stata for Behavioural Research*. Emerald Group Publishing.

Rapoport, A., D. G. Gordon, and M. J. Guyer (1976). *The 2x2 Game*. U of Michigan P.

Rapoport, A. and M. Guyer (1966). A taxonomy of 2 x 2 games. *General Systems 11*, 203–214.

Richardson, L. F. (1919). The mathematical psychology of war.

Richardson, L. F. (1960a). *Arms and Insecurity*. Chicago: Quadrangle Books.

Richardson, L. F. (1960b). *Statistics of Deadly Quarrels*. Chicago: Quadrangle Books.

Robinson, D. and D. Goforth (2005). The topology of 2x2 games: A new periodic table.

Sandler, T. (2004). *Global collective action*. Cambridge, England: Cambridge University Press.

Schelling, T. C. (1960). *The Strategy of Conflict*. Cambridge (Mass.): Harvard UP.

Schramm, H. C. and D. P. Gaver (2013). Lanchester for cyber: the mixed epidemic-combat model. *Naval Research Logistics 60*, 599–605.

Washburn, A. and M. Kress (2009). *Combat Modeling*. Heidelberg: Springer.